*Early Translation of the
Acts of the Apostles*

By Luke

Copyright © 2021 Lamp of Trismegistus. All rights reserved. No part of this publication may be reproduced or transmitted in any form or by any means, electronic or mechanical, including photocopying, recording, or by any information storage and retrieval system, without permission in writing from Lamp of Trismegistus. Reviewers may quote brief passages.

ISBN: 978-1-63118-521-2

Christian Apocrypha Series

Other Books in this Series and Related Titles

The Book of Wisdom of Solomon by King Solomon (978-1-63118-502-1)

The Gospel of the Nativity of Mary by St. Matthew (978-1-63118-448-2)

The Hymn of Jesus by G. R. S. Mead (978-1-63118-409-3)

The Vision of Saint Paul the Apostle by Paul (978-1-63118-526-7)

The First and Second Gospels of the Infancy of Jesus Christ (978-1-63118-415-4)

The Book of Parables by Enoch (978-1-63118-429-1)

The Testament of Abraham by Abraham (978-1-63118-441-3)

The Lives of Adam and Eve by Moses (978-1-63118-414-7)

Psalms of Solomon by King Solomon (978-1-63118-439-0)

Masonic Symbolism of King Solomon's Temple by A Mackey &c (978-1-63118-442-0)

The Secrets of Enoch by Enoch (978-1-63118-449-9)

Lost Chapters of the Book of Daniel and Related Writings (978-1-63118-417-8)

The Testament of Moses by Moses (978-1-63118-440-6)

The Book of the Watchers by Enoch (978-1-63118-416-1)

Buddhist Psalms by Shinran (978-1-63118-465-9)

Masonic Symbolism of Easter and the Christ in Masonry (978-1-63118-434-5)

The Odes of Solomon by King Solomon (978-1-63118-503-8)

Book of Dreams by Enoch (978-1-63118-437-6)

The Apocalypse of Peter by Peter (978-1-63118-527-4)

The Hymns of Hermes by G. R. S. Mead (978-1-63118-405-5)

The Book of Astronomical Secrets by Enoch (978-1-63118-443-7)

Audio Versions are also Available on Audible, Amazon and Apple

INTRODUCTION

The Apocrypha are a loosely knit series of books, written by early vanguards of Christianity (covering the eras of both the old and new testaments), and which comprise somewhere between about a dozen to several hundred titles, depending on whom you ask and how that person defines "Apocrypha." A small selection of these can still be found included in the Catholic bible, while a majority of the books in question, were abandoned by church officials in the early centuries of Christianity. Many of these apocryphal books were originally considered canon by early followers of Christ, in the first four centuries following his birth. It wasn't until the meeting of the Council of Nicaea in 325, that Emperor Constantine and a group of roughly 300 church bishops, gathered together with the goal of defining, standardizing and unifying an otherwise splintering Christianity, that many of these writings ceased to be included in the newly established canon. Enjoy then, this book as an example, of just one of the many books of the Christian Apocrypha, and be sure to check out other titles in this series.

NOTE ON THE TRANSLATION THAT FOLLOWS

The sole object of publishing this translation of the Greek text of so much of the *Acts of the Apostles* as has survived in the *Codex Bezae* is to enable the English reader to form a judgment, based on internal and literary evidence alone, as to the relation between the original source of this text, and that of the shorter text from which our A.V. and R.V. are translated.[1] It is my belief that a careful examination of it will do more than suggest to the reader as possible, it will convince him of the fact, that we have before us traces of the revision of a work by the author himself, the words in **bold type** being struck by him out of his first draft, and the words in [square brackets] introduced. The other argument, based on external and historical evidence, pointing to the same conclusion, is also briefly alluded to in the Introduction.

This being the sole object of the translation, it will, I hope, be understood that this is not a critical collation of texts, and deals with no other critical question. Many obvious errors of transcription in the MS. are tacitly corrected. In some rewritten passages the whole is in thick type though parts of them appear in the ordinary text. The reader is assumed to have the R.V. open before him, or in his memory. The translation is in general that of the R.V. or its margin.

I have, in a word, endeavoured to put before the English reader the purely literary question----revision by author or interpolation by copyist----in a form at once fair and simple and readable.

---

[1] A.V and R.V. are both early abbreviations meaning, what today would be simply called the *King James Version* or K.J.V.

CHAPTER I

The former treatise I made, O Theophilus, concerning all that Jesus began both to do and to teach, until the day in which he was received up, after that he had given commandment through the Holy Spirit unto the apostles whom he had chosen, **and ordered to proclaim the gospel:** to whom he also shewed himself alive after his passion by many proofs, appearing unto them by the space of forty days, and speaking the things concerning the kingdom of God: and, being assembled together with them, he charged them not to depart from Jerusalem, but to wait for the promise of the Father, which ye heard, **saith he, from my mouth:** for John indeed baptized with water; but ye shall be baptized with the Holy Spirit, **and which ye are about to receive** after these not many days **until the Pentecost.**

They therefore, when they were come together, asked him, saying, Lord, dost thou at this time restore the kingdom of Israel? And he said unto them, It is not for you to know times or seasons, which the Father hath set within his own authority. But ye shall receive power, when the Holy Spirit is come upon you; and ye shall be my witnesses both in Jerusalem, and in all Judaea and Samaria, and unto the uttermost part of the earth. And when he had said these things, [as they were looking], a cloud received him, and he was taken away out of their sight. And while they were looking stedfastly into heaven as he went, behold, two men stood by them in white apparel; which also said, Ye men of Galilee, why stand ye looking into heaven? this Jesus, which was received up from you [into heaven], shall so come in like manner as ye beheld him going into heaven.

Then returned they unto Jerusalem from the mount called Olivet, which is nigh unto Jerusalem, a sabbath day's journey off.

And when they were come in, they went up into the upper chamber, where they were abiding; both Peter and John, [and] James and Andrew, Philip and Thomas, Bartholomew and Matthew, James of Alphaeus, [and] Simon the Zealot, and Judas of James. These all with one accord continued stedfastly in prayer, with **the** women **and children**, and Mary the mother of Jesus, and [with] his brethren.

And in these days Peter stood up in the midst of the **disciples,** and said (**for** there was a multitude of persons together about a hundred and twenty), **Men and** brethren, it was needful that **this** scripture should be fulfilled, which the Holy Spirit spake before by the mouth of David concerning Judas, who was guide to them that took Jesus.

For he was numbered among us, and received his portion in this ministry. Now this man obtained a field with the reward of his iniquity; and falling headlong he burst asunder in the midst, and all his bowels gushed out. And it became known to all the dwellers at Jerusalem; insomuch that in their language that field was called Akeldamach, that is, The field of blood,

For it is written in the book of Psalms,

Let his habitation be made desolate,
And let no man dwell therein:
And his overseership let another take.

Of the men therefore which have companied with us all the time that the Lord Jesus **Christ** went in and went out among us, beginning from the baptism of John, unto the day that he was received up from us, of these must one become a witness with us of his resurrection. And **he** put forward two, Joseph called **Barnabas**, who was surnamed Justus, and Matthias. And they prayed, and said, Thou, Lord, which knowest the hearts of all men, shew of these two the one whom thou hast chosen, to take the place in this ministry and apostleship, from which Judas fell away, that he might go to his own place. And they gave lots for them; and the lot fell upon Matthias; and he was numbered with the **twelve** apostles.

CHAPTER II

And **it came to pass in those days** of the fulfilment of the day of the Pentecost, when they were all [together] in one place, and, **behold**, suddenly there came from heaven a sound as of a rushing mighty wind, and it filled all the house where they were sitting. And there appeared unto them tongues parting asunder, like as of fire: and **they** sat upon each one of them. And they were all filled with the Holy Spirit, and began to speak with other tongues, as the Spirit gave them utterance.

[Now] there were dwelling in Jerusalem Jews, devout men, from every nation under heaven. And when this sound took place, the multitude came together, and were confounded; **and** each one heard them speaking in their own **tongues**. And they were [all] amazed and marvelled, saying to one another, Behold are not all these which speak Galilaeans? And how hear we each one our own language wherein we were born? Parthians and Medes and Elamites, and dwellers in Mesopotamia, Judaea and Cappadocia, in Pontus and Asia, in Phrygia and Pamphylia, in Egypt and the parts of Libya about Cyrene, and sojourners from Rome, both Jews and proselytes, Cretans and Arabians, we do hear them speaking in our tongues the mighty works of God. And they were all amazed, and were perplexed, one with another, **about what had taken place, and** saying What meaneth this? but others mocking said, They are filled with new wine.

But then Peter, standing up with the **ten apostles,** lifted up his voice **first,** and **said,** Ye men of Judaea, and all ye that dwell at Jerusalem, be this known unto **us,** [and] give ear unto my words. For these are not drunken, as ye suppose; seeing it is but the third hour of the day: but this is that which hath been spoken by the prophet [Joel]:

> [And] it shall be in the last days, saith the Lord,
> I will pour forth of my Spirit upon all flesh;
> And **their** sons and **their** daughters shall prophesy,
> And **the** young men shall see visions,
> And **the** old men shall dream dreams;
> [yea] and on my servants and on my hand maidens [in those days]
> I will pour out of my Spirit;
> [And they shall prophesy].
> And I will shew wonders in the heaven above,
> and signs on the earth beneath,
> [blood, and fire, and vapour of smoke].
> the sun shall be turned into darkness,
> and the moon into blood,
> before the day of the Lord come,
> that great [and notable day].
> And it shall be, that whosoever shall call on the name
> of the Lord shall be saved.

Ye men of Israel, hear these words, Jesus of Nazareth, a man approved of God unto **us** by mighty works and wonders and signs, which God did by him in the midst of you, even as ye yourselves know; him, being delivered up by the determinate counsel and foreknowledge of God, ye **took, and** by the hand of lawless men did crucify and slay; whom God raised up, having loosed the pains of **Hades,** because it was not possible that he should be holden of it. For David saith concerning him,

> I beheld **my** Lord always before my face;
> For he is on my right hand, that I should not be moved;
> Therefore my heart was glad, and my tongue rejoiced;
> Moreover my flesh also shall dwell in hope:
> Because thou wilt not leave my soul in Hades,
> Neither wilt thou give thy Holy One to see corruption.

Thou madest known unto me the ways of life;
Thou shalt make me full of gladness with thy countenance.

Men and brethren, I may say unto you freely of the patriarch David, that he both died and was buried, and his tomb is with us unto this day. Being therefore a prophet, and knowing that God had sworn with an oath to him, that of the fruit of **his heart according to the flesh he would raise up the Christ**, and set him upon his throne: [he foreseeing this spake] of the resurrection of the Christ, that neither was he left in Hades, nor did his flesh see corruption. This Jesus **therefore** did God raise up, whereof we all are witnesses. Being therefore by the right hand of God exalted, and having received of the Father the promise of the Holy Spirit, he hath poured forth upon you this, which ye **both** see and hear. For David ascended not into the heavens; for he **said** himself

The Lord said unto my Lord,
Sit thou on my right hand,
Till I make thine enemies
The footstool of thy feet.

Let all the house of Israel know assuredly that God hath made [him] both Lord and Christ, this Jesus whom ye crucified.

Then all **who had come together**, when they heard this, were pricked in their heart, and **some of them** said to Peter and the [rest of the] apostles, **Men and** brethren, what **therefore** shall we do? **Shew us.** And Peter saith unto them, Repent ye, and be baptized every one of you in the name of the **Lord** Jesus Christ unto the Remission of [your] sins; and ye shall receive the gift of the Holy Spirit. For to **us** is the promise, and to **our** children, and to all that are afar off, even as many as the Lord our God shall call unto him. And with many other words he testified, and exhorted them, saying, Save yourselves from this crooked generation. They then that **believed** his word were baptized; and there were added [unto them] in that day about three thousand souls. And they continued stedfastly in the apostles' teaching **in Jerusalem,** and the fellowship, in the breaking of the bread, and the prayers. And fear came upon every soul: and many wonders and signs were done by the Apostles. And all that believed were together, and had all things common; and **as many as** had possessions or goods sold them, and parted them **day by day** to all those who had need. And **all** continued stedfastly [with one accord], in the temple, and in their homes together breaking bread they did take their food with gladness and singleness of heart, praising God, and having favour with all the **world.** And the Lord added [to them] those that were being saved day by day **together in the Church.**

CHAPTER III

Now in those days Peter and John were going up into the temple **in the evening** at the ninth hour, that of prayer. And, **behold,** a certain man, that was lame from his mother's womb was being carried, whom they laid daily at the door of the temple which is called Beautiful, to ask alms of them that were entering into the temple. **He fixing steadily his eyes, and** seeing Peter and John about to go into the temple, asked alms **from them.** And Peter, looking on him, with John, said, Look **steadily** on us. And he **looked steadily on them,** expecting to receive something from them. But Peter said, Silver and gold have I none; but what I have, that give I thee. In the name of Jesus Christ of Nazareth, walk. And he took him by the right hand, and raised him up. And immediately **he stood; and** his feet and ankle-bones received strength. And leaping up, he stood, and walked **rejoicing,** and entered with them into the temple [walking, and leaping, and] praising God: And all the people saw him walking and praising God. And they took knowledge of him, that it was he which sat for alms at the Beautiful Gate of the temple; and they were filled with wonder and amazement at that which had happened unto him.

And **as Peter and John went out,** he **went out with them, and** held them: and [all the people ran together unto them and] were **standing** astonished in the porch that is called Solomon's, greatly wondering. But Peter answering said unto them: Ye men of Israel, why marvel ye at this? or why fasten ye your eyes on us, as though by our own power or godliness we had done **this thing** that he should walk? The God of Abraham and **the God** of Isaac, and **the God** of Jacob, the God of our fathers hath glorified his servant Jesus **Christ,** whom ye delivered up **to judgment,** and denied him before the face of Pilate, when he had **judged and**

wished to release him. But ye **oppressed** the Holy and Righteous One, and asked for a murderer to be granted unto you. And ye killed the Prince of life; whom God raised from the dead; whereof we are witnesses. And by faith in his name **ye behold this man and know that his name made him strong,** and the faith which is by him hath given him this perfect soundness in the presence of you all. And now, **men** and **brethren, we** know that ye did **a wicked thing** in ignorance, as did also your rulers. But the things which God foreshewed by the mouth of all the prophets, that his Christ should suffer, he hath thus fulfilled. Repent ye therefore, and turn again, that your sins may be blotted out, that so there may come seasons of refreshing from the face of the Lord; and that he may send the Christ who hath been appointed for you, even Jesus, whom the heaven must receive until the times of restoration of all things, whereof God spake by the mouth of his holy prophets [which have been since the world began.] Moses indeed said **unto our fathers,** A prophet shall the Lord your God raise up unto you of our brethren; to him **like unto myself** shall ye hearken in all things whatsoever he shall speak unto you. And it shall be, that every soul, which shall not hearken to that prophet, shall be utterly destroyed from among the people. Yea, and all the prophets, from Samuel and them that followed after, as many as have spoken, they also told of these days. Ye are the sons of the prophets, and of the covenant which God made with your fathers, saying unto Abraham, And in thy seed shall all the families of the earth be blessed. Unto you first, God having raised up his Servant, sent him to bless you, in turning away every one of you from your iniquities.

CHAPTER IV

And as they spake **these words** unto the people, the priests and [the captain of the temple] and the Sadducees came upon them, being sore troubled because they taught the people, and proclaimed **Jesus in the resurrection of the dead.** And they laid hands on them, and put them in ward unto the morrow: for it was now eventide. But many of them that heard the word believed; and the number **also** of the men came to be about five thousand.

And it came to pass on the **day of the** morrow, that **the** rulers and elders and Scribes were gathered together in Jerusalem; and Annas the high-priest, and Caiaphas, and **Jonathas** and Alexander, and as many as were of the kindred of the high-priest. And when they had set them in the midst, they inquired, By what power, or in what name, have ye done this? Then Peter, filled with the Holy Spirit, said unto them, Ye rulers of the people, and elders of **Israel,** if we this day are examined **by you** concerning a good deed done to an impotent man, by what means this man is made whole; be it known unto you all, and to all the people of Israel, that in the name of Jesus Christ of Nazareth, whom ye crucified, whom God raised from the dead, in him doth this man stand here before you whole. He is the stone which was set at nought of you the builders, which was made the head of the corner. And in none other is there [salvation], for there is none other name under heaven given **to** men, wherein we must be saved.

Now when they beheld the boldness of Peter and John, and had perceived that they were unlearned [and ignorant] men, they marvelled; but they took knowledge of them, that they had been with Jesus. [And] seeing the man that was healed standing with them, they could **do or** say nothing against it. [But] when they had commanded that they **should be led** out of the Council, they conferred among themselves, saying, What shall we do to these men? for that indeed a notable sign hath been wrought through them is **more than** manifest to all that dwell in Jerusalem, and we cannot deny it. [But] that it spread no further among the people, let us threaten them, that they speak henceforth to no man in this name. And **when they had agreed to this decision** they called them, and charged them not to speak [at all] nor teach in the name of Jesus. But Peter and John answered and said unto them, Whether it be right in the sight of God to hearken unto you rather than unto God, judge ye: for we cannot **[but]** speak the things which we saw and heard. And they, when they had further threatened them, let them go, finding nothing how they might punish them, because of the people; for all men glorified God for that which was done. For the man was more than forty years old, on whom this sign of healing was wrought.

And being let go, they came to their own company, and reported all that the chief priests and the elders had said unto them. And they, when they heard it, **and recognised the working of God,** lifted up their voice to God with one accord, and said, O Lord, thou **the God** that didst make the heaven and the earth and the sea, and all that in them is: who by the Holy Spirit, by the mouth of [our father] David thy servant didst say,

Why did the Gentiles rage,
And the peoples imagine vain things?
The kings of the earth set themselves in array,
And the rulers were gathered together,
Against the Lord, and against his Anointed:

For of a truth in this city, against thy holy Servant Jesus, whom thou didst anoint, both Herod and Pontius Pilate were gathered together with the Gentiles and the peoples of Israel, to do whatsoever thy hand and thy counsel foreordained to come to pass.

And now, Lord, look upon their threatenings: and grant unto thy servants to speak thy word with all boldness, while thou stretchest forth thy hand to heal, and that signs and wonders may be done through the name of thy holy Servant Jesus. And when they had prayed, the place was shaken wherein they were gathered together: and they were all filled with the Holy Spirit, and they spake the word of God with boldness, **to every man who wished to believe.**

And the multitude of them that believed were of one heart and soul, **and there was no distinction at all** among them: and not one of them said that aught of the things which he possessed was his own; but they had all things common. And with great power gave the apostles their witness of the resurrection of the Lord Jesus **Christ;** and great grace was upon them all. For neither was there among them any that lacked; for as many as were possessed of lands or houses sold them, and brought the prices of the things that were sold, and laid them at the apostles' feet : and distribution was made unto each **one** according as anyone had need.

And Joseph, who by the apostles was surnamed Barnabas, (which is, being interpreted, Son of Exhortation), a **Cyprian Levite** by race, having a field sold it, and brought the money, and laid it at the apostles' feet.

CHAPTER V

But a certain man named Ananias, with Sapphira his wife, sold a possession and kept back part of the price, his wife also being privy to it, and brought a certain part, and laid it at the apostles' feet. But Peter said **to** Ananias, Why hath Satan filled thy heart to lie to the Holy Spirit, to keep back part of the price of the land? Whiles it remained, did it not remain thine own? and after it was sold was it not in thy power? How is it that thou hast conceived in thy heart **to do** this **wicked** thing? thou hast not lied unto men but unto God. And when he heard these words Ananias **immediately** fell down and gave up the ghost, and great fear came upon all that heard it. And the young men arose and wrapped him round, and they carried him out and buried him.

And it was about the space of three hours after when his wife, not knowing what was done, came in. And Peter **said** to her **I will further ask you if verily** ye sold the land for so much. She **then** said, Yea, for so much. But Peter (said) unto her, How is it that ye have agreed together to tempt the Spirit of the Lord? Behold, the feet of them which have buried thy husband are at the door, and they shall carry thee out. And she fell down immediately at his feet, and gave up the ghost. And the young men came in, and found her dead; and **having wrapped her round** they carried her out, and buried her by her husband. And great fear fell upon the whole church, and upon all that heard these things.

And by the hands of the apostles were many signs and wonders wrought among the people; and they were all with one accord **in the temple** in Solomon's porch. But of the rest durst no one join himself to them; howbeit the people magnified them. And were the more added to them, believing on the Lord, multitudes both of men and women: insomuch that they [even] carried out **their** sick into the streets, and laid them on beds and couches, that, as Peter came by, at the least his shadow might overshadow some one of them. **For they were set free from every sickness which each one of them had.** And there came [also] together into Jerusalem a multitude from the cities round about, bringing sick folk, and them that were vexed with unclean spirits: and all were **cured**.

But the high priest rose up, and all they that were with him which is the sect of the Sadducees, and they were filled with jealousy; and laid hands on the apostles, and put them in public ward: **and each one of them went to his own home. Then** by night an angel of the Lord opened the doors of the prison, and brought them out, and said, Go and stand and speak in the temple to the people all the words of this Life. And when they heard this, they entered into the temple about day break, and taught. But the high priest came, and they that were with him, **having been roused early,** and called the council together, and all the senate of the children of Israel, and sent to the prison to have them brought. But the officers having come **and opened the prison** found them not within; and they returned, and told, saying, The prison-house we found shut in all safety, and the keepers standing at the doors; but when we had opened we found no man within. Now when the captain of the temple and the chief priests heard these words, they were much perplexed concerning them whereunto this would grow. And there came one and told them, Behold the men whom ye put in the prison are in the temple, standing and teaching the people. Then went the captain with the officers, and brought them [not] with violence: for they feared the people, lest they should be stoned. And when they had brought them they set them before the Council. And the [high] priest asked them, saying, **Did we not** straitly charge you not to teach in this name? And, behold, ye have filled Jerusalem with your teaching, and wish to bring that man's blood upon us. But Peter [and the apostles answered and] said **to them,** We must obey God rather than men. The God of our fathers raised up Jesus, whom ye slew, hanging him on a tree. Him did God exalt **for his glory** [with his right hand], to be a Prince and a Saviour, to give repentance to Israel, and remission of sins **in him.** And we are witnesses of **all** these things; and so is the Holy Spirit, whom God hath given to them that obey him.

But they, when they heard this, were cut to the heart, and were minded to slay them. But there stood up one of the council, a Pharisee, named Gamaliel, a doctor of the law, had in honour of all the people, and commanded to put **the apostles** forth a little while. And he said **to the rulers and those of the council,** Ye men of Israel, take heed to yourselves as touching these men, what ye are about to do. For before these days rose up Theudas, giving himself out to be somebody **great**: to whom a number of men, about four hundred, joined themselves; who was slain **by himself,** and all as many as obeyed him, and came to nought. After this man rose up Judas of Galilee, in the days of the enrolment, and drew away **much** people after him: he also perished, and all, as many as obeyed him, were scattered abroad. And now, **brethren; I** say unto you, Refrain from these men, and let them alone, **not defiling your hands;** for if this counsel or this work be of men, it will be overthrown; but if it is of God, ye will not be able to hinder them: **neither you nor kings nor tyrants: keep away therefore from these men,** lest haply ye be found fighting against God. And to him they agreed: and when they had called the apostles unto them, they beat them, and charged them not to speak in the name of Jesus, and let them go. The **apostles** therefore departed from the presence of the Council, rejoicing that they were counted worthy to suffer dishonour for the Name. And every day, in the temple and at home they ceased not to teach and preach the **Lord** Jesus as the Christ.

CHAPTER VI

Now in these days, when the number of the disciples was multiplying, there arose a murmuring of the Hellenists against the Hebrews, because their widows were neglected in the daily ministration, **in the ministration of the Hebrews.** [And] the twelve called the multitude of the disciples unto them, and said, It is not pleasing to us that we should leave the word of God, and minister to tables. **What is it then,** brethren? Look ye out [therefore] from among you seven men of good report, full of the Spirit and of wisdom, whom we will appoint over this business: but we will continue stedfastly in prayer, and in the ministry of the word. And **this** saying pleased the whole multitude **of the disciples;** and they chose Stephen, a man full of faith and of the Holy Spirit, and Philip, and Prochorus, and **Nicor,** and Timon, and Parmenas, and Nicolas a proselyte of Antioch. **These** were set before the apostles; and when they had prayed, they laid their hands on them. And the word of the Lord increased; and the number of the disciples multiplied in Jerusalem exceedingly; and a great company of the priests were obedient to the faith. And Stephen, full of grace and power, wrought great wonders and signs among the people, **through the name of the Lord Jesus Christ.** But there arose certain of them that were of the Synagogue called the Synagogue of the Libertines, and of the Cyrenians, and of the Alexandrians, and of them of Cilicia [and Asia] disputing with Stephen. And they were not able to withstand the wisdom **that was in him,** and the **Holy** Spirit with which he spake, **because they were confuted by him with all boldness. Being unable therefore to face the truth** then they suborned men which said, We have heard him speak blasphemous words against Moses, and against God, And they stirred up the people, and the elders, and the scribes, and came upon him, and seized him, and brought him into the Council; and set up false witnesses **against him,** which said, This man ceaseth not to speak words against **the** holy place, and the law: for we have heard him say that this Jesus of Nazareth shall destroy this place, and shall change the customs which Moses delivered unto us. And all that sat in the council, fastening their eyes on him, saw his face as it had been the face of an angel **standing in the midst of them.**

CHAPTER VII

And the high priest said **to Stephen, Is this thing** so? And he said **Men,** brethren and fathers, hearken. The God of glory appeared to our father Abraham, when he was in Mesopotamia, before he dwelt in Haran, and said unto him, Get thee out of thy land, and from thy kindred, and come into the land which I shall shew thee. Then came **Abraham** out of the land of the Chaldeans, and dwelt in Haran; and **there he was** after the death of his father. And (God) removed him into this land, wherein ye now dwell, **and our fathers who were before us.** And he gave him none inheritance in it, no, not so much as to set his foot on: **but** he promised that he would give it him in possession, and his seed after him, when as yet he had no child. And God spake on this wise **to him,** that his seed should sojourn in a strange land, and that they should bring them into bondage, and entreat them evil, four hundred years. And the nation to which they shall be in bondage will I judge, said God, and after that shall they come forth, and serve me in this place. And he gave him the covenant of circumcision. And so he begat Isaac, and circumcised him the eighth day; and Isaac begat Jacob, and Jacob the twelve patriarchs. And the patriarchs, moved with jealousy against Joseph, sold him into Egypt; and God was with him, and delivered him out of all his afflictions, and gave him favour and wisdom before Pharaoh, King of Egypt; and he made him governor over Egypt and all his house. Now there came a famine over all Egypt and Canaan, and great affliction; and our fathers found no sustenance. When **therefore** Jacob heard that there was corn in Egypt, he sent forth our fathers the first time. And at the second time Joseph was made known to his brethren, and Joseph's race became manifest unto Pharaoh. And Joseph sent, and called to him Jacob his father and all his kindred, three score and fifteen souls. And Jacob went down into Egypt; and he died, himself, and our fathers. And they were carried over unto Shechem, and laid in the tomb that Abraham bought for a price in silver of the sons of Emmor of Shechem. But as the time of the promise drew nigh, which God **promised** unto Abraham, the people grew and multiplied in Egypt, till there arose another king [over Egypt] which knew not Joseph. The same dealt subtilly with our race, and evil entreated **the** fathers, that they should cast out their babes to the end they might not live.

At which season Moses was born, and was exceeding fair; and he was nourished three months in his father's house. And when he was cast out **by the riverside,** Pharaoh's daughter took him up and nourished him for her own son. And Moses was instructed in all the wisdom of the Egyptians, and he was mighty in his words and works. But when he was full forty years old it came into his heart to visit his brethren the children of Israel. And seeing one **of his race** suffering wrong, he defended him, and avenged him that was oppressed, smiting the Egyptian, **and he hid him in the sand;** and he supposed that his brethren understood how that God by his hand was giving them deliverance; but they understood not. And **then** on the day following he appeared unto them as they strove, **and saw them doing injustice,** and would have set them at one again, saying, **What are ye doing,** men and brethren? why do ye wrong one to another? But he that did his neighbour wrong thrust him away saying, Who made thee a ruler and a judge over us? Wouldest thou kill me as thou killedst the Egyptian yesterday? **Thus also** Moses fled at this saying, and became a sojourner in the land of Midian, where he begat two sons.

And **after these things,** when forty years were fulfilled, an angel **of the Lord** appeared to him in the wilderness of Mount Sinai, in a flame of fire in a bush. And when Moses saw it, he wondered at the sight: and as he drew near to behold, the Lord **spake to**

him saying, I am the God of thy fathers, the God of Abraham, and **the God** of Isaac, and **the God** of Jacob. And Moses trembled, and durst not behold. And **a voice** came to him, Loose the shoes from thy feet: for the place whereon thou standest is holy ground. I have surely seen the affliction of my people which is in Egypt, and have heard their groaning, and I am come down to deliver them: and now come, I will send thee into Egypt.

This Moses whom they refused, saying, Who made thee a ruler and a judge **over us,** him hath God sent to be both a ruler and a redeemer with the hand of the angel which appeared to him in the bush. This man led them forth, having wrought wonders and signs in Egypt, and in the Red Sea, and in the wilderness forty years. This is [that] Moses, which said unto the children of Israel, A prophet shall God raise up unto you from among your brethren, as he raised up me: **hear him.** This is he that was in the church in the wilderness with the angel which spake to him in the mount Sinai, and **of** our fathers; who received living oracles to give unto us: **because** our fathers would not be obedient, but thrust him from them, and turned back in their hearts unto Egypt, saying unto Aaron, Make us gods which shall go before us: for as for this Moses, which led us forth out of the land of Egypt, we wot not what is become of him. And they made a calf in those days, and brought a sacrifice unto the idol, and rejoiced in the works of their hands. But God turned, and gave them up to serve the host of heaven; as it is written in the book of the prophets, Did ye offer unto me slain beasts and sacrifices, forty years in the wilderness, O house of Israel? And ye took up the tabernacle of Moloch, and the star of the god Remphan, the figures which ye made to worship them; and I will carry you away into **the parts** of Babylon. The tabernacle of the testimony was with our fathers in the wilderness, even as he appointed who spake unto Moses that he should make it according to the figure that he had seen. Which also our fathers, in their turn, brought in with Joshua when they entered on the possession of the nations, which God thrust out before the face of our fathers, unto the days of David; who found favour in the sight of God, and asked to find a habitation for the **house** of Jacob. But Solomon built him a house. Howbeit the Most High dwelleth not in houses made with hands, as saith the prophet, The heaven is my throne, and the earth the footstool of my feet. What manner of house will ye build me? saith the Lord: or of **what sort** is the place of my rest ? Did not my hand make all these things? Ye stiffnecked and uncircumcised in heart and ears, ye do always resist the Holy Spirit: as your fathers did, so do ye. Which of the prophets did not they persecute? and they killed them which shewed before of the coming of the Righteous One; of whom ye have now become betrayers and murderers; ye who received the law as it was ordained by angels, and kept it not.

Now when they heard these things, they were cut to the heart, and they gnashed on him with their teeth. But he, being full of the Holy Spirit, looked up stedfastly into heaven, and saw the glory of God, and Jesus **the Lord,** standing on the right hand of God: and said, Behold I see the heavens opened, and the Son of Man standing on the right hand of God. But they cried out with a loud voice, and stopped their ears, and rushed upon him with one accord; and they cast him out of the city, and stoned him ; and the witnesses laid down their garments at the feet **of** a **certain** young man named Saul. And they stoned Stephen calling upon [the Lord] and saying, Lord Jesus, receive my spirit. And he kneeled down, and cried with a loud voice, **saying,** Lord, lay not this sin to their charge; and when he had said this, he fell asleep.

CHAPTER VIII

And Saul was consenting unto his death.

And there arose on that day a great persecution **and affliction** against the church which was in Jerusalem; and they were all scattered abroad throughout the regions of Judaea and Samaria, except the apostles, **who remained in Jerusalem.** And devout men buried Stephen, and made great lamentation over him. But Saul laid waste the church, entering into every house, and haling men and women, committed them to prison.

They therefore that were scattered abroad went about preaching the word. And Philip went down to the city of Samaria, and proclaimed unto them the Christ. And, **when they heard,** all the multitudes gave heed unto the things which were spoken by Philip with one accord, when they heard and saw the signs which he did. For from many of those which had unclean spirits they came out crying with a loud voice, and many that were palsied [and that were] lame were healed. And there was much joy in that city. But there was a certain man, Simon by name, which beforetime in the city used sorcery, and amazed the people of Samaria, giving out that he himself was some great one ; to whom they all gave heed from the least to the greatest, saying, This man is the power of God which is called Great. And they gave heed to him, because that of long time he had amazed them with his sorceries. But when they believed Philip preaching good tidings concerning the kingdom of God and the name of Jesus Christ, they were baptized, both men and women. And Simon also himself believed, and **was** baptized, and he continued with Philip; and beholding signs and great miracles wrought, he was amazed. Now when the apostles which were at Jerusalem heard that Samaria had received the word of God, they sent unto them Peter and John; who when they were come down, prayed for them, that they might receive the Holy Spirit: for as yet he was fallen upon none of them: only they had been baptized into the name of the Lord Jesus **Christ**. Then laid they their hands upon them, and they received the Holy Spirit. Now when Simon saw that through the laying on of the apostles' hands the Holy Spirit was given, he brought them money, **exhorting them** and saying, Give me also this power, that on whomsoever **I also** lay my hands, he may receive the Holy Spirit. But Peter said unto him, Thy silver perish with thee, because thou hast thought to obtain the gift of God with money. Thou hast neither part nor lot in this matter, for thy heart is not right before God. Repent therefore from this thy wickedness, and pray the Lord if perhaps the thought of thy heart shall be forgiven thee: for I see that thou art in the gall of bitterness and in the bond of iniquity. And Simon answered and said **to them I beseech you** pray ye for me to **God** that none of these **evils of** which ye have spoken come upon me. **And he ceased not to shed** many **tears.**

They therefore, when they had testified and spoken the word of the Lord, returned to Jerusalem, and preached the gospel to many villages of the Samaritans.

But an angel of the Lord spake unto Philip saying, Arise, and go toward the south unto the way that goeth down from Jerusalem unto Gaza: the same is desert. And he arose and went: and, behold, a man of Ethiopia, an eunuch of great authority under Candace, **a certain** queen of the Ethiopians, who had the charge of all her treasure, who had come to Jerusalem for to worship: and he was returning and sitting in his chariot [and was] reading the prophet Isaiah. And the Spirit said unto Philip...

Here eight leaves of the Codex are wanting, including from viii. 29 to x. 14 in Greek, and viii. 20 to x. 4 in Latin. The Latin text, d, follows a from x. 4 to x. 14. The following chapter consequently jumps to X.

29

CHAPTER X

...anything that is common or unclean **and called** unto him again the second time, What God hath cleansed, make not thou common. And this was done thrice: and [straight way] the vessel was received up **again** into heaven. Now **when** he came **to himself** Peter doubted what this vision which he had seen should mean: and, behold the men that were sent **from** Cornelius, having made enquiry for Simon's house, stood before the gate, and called and asked whether Simon, which was surnamed Peter, was lodging there. And while Peter thought on the vision, the Spirit said unto him, Behold [three] men seek thee. But arise, and get thee down, and go with them nothing doubting; for I have sent them. **Then** Peter went down to the men and said, Behold I am he whom ye seek. **What do you wish?** or what is the cause wherefore ye are come? And they said **to him,** A **certain** Cornelius, a centurion, a righteous man, and one that feareth God, and well reported of by all the nation of the Jews, was warned by a holy angel to send for thee into his house, and to hear words from thee. Then **Peter led** them in and lodged them.

And on the morrow he arose and went forth with them, and certain of the brethren from Joppa accompanied him. And on the morrow **he** entered into Caesarea. And Cornelius **was expecting them,** and having called together his kinsmen and his near friends he was waiting for them. **And as Peter was drawing near to Caesarea one of the servants ran forward and announced that he was come. And Cornelius sprang up and** met him, and fell down at his feet, and worshipped him. But Peter raised him up saying **What art thou doing?** I myself also am a man **as thou also art.** And [as he talked with him] he went in, and found many come together. And he said unto them, Ye yourselves know **very**

well how that it is an unlawful thing for a man that is a Jew to join himself or come unto one that is of another nation: and unto me hath God shewed that I should not call any man common or unclean. Wherefore also I came without gainsaying when I was sent for **by you.** I ask therefore with what intent ye sent for me. And Cornelius said, **From the third day** until this hour **I was fasting,** and keeping the ninth hour of prayer in my house, and behold, a man stood before me in bright apparel, and saith, Cornelius, thy prayer is heard, and thine alms are had in remembrance in the sight of God. Send therefore to Joppa, and call unto thee Simon, who is surnamed Peter; he lodgeth in the house of Simon a tanner by the seaside. **He when he cometh shall speak unto thee.** Forthwith therefore I sent to thee **exhorting thee to come unto us;** and thou hast well done that thou hast come with speed. Now therefore we all in thy sight are wishing to hear **from thee** that which has been commanded thee by **God.**

And Peter opened his mouth and said, Of a truth I perceive that God is no respecter of persons; but in every nation he that feareth him, and worketh righteousness, is acceptable to him. **For** the word which he sent unto the children of Israel, preaching good tidings of peace by Jesus Christ, (he is Lord of all), ye know that [saying] which took place throughout all Judaea; **for** beginning from Galilee, after the baptism which John preached, even Jesus of Nazareth, whom God anointed with the Holy Spirit and with power. He went about doing good, and healing all that were oppressed of the devil; for God was with him. And we are **his** witnesses of [all] the things which he did both in the country of the Jews, and in Jerusalem; whom also they slew, hanging him on a tree. Him God raised up **after** the third day, and gave him to be made manifest, not to all the people, but unto witnesses that were chosen before of God, even to us, who did eat and drink with him, **and companied with him,** after he rose from the dead **for**

forty days. And he charged us to preach unto the people, and to testify that this is he which is ordained of God to be the Judge of quick and dead. To him bear all the prophets witness, that through his name every one that believeth on him shall receive remission of sins.

While Peter yet spake these words, the Holy Spirit fell on all them that heard the word. And they of the circumcision which believed were amazed, as many as came with Peter, because that on the Gentiles also was poured out the gift of the Holy Spirit. For they heard them speak with uncertain tongues and magnify God. And Peter said, Can any man forbid the water, that these should not be baptized, which have received the Holy Spirit as well as we? Then he commanded them to be baptized in the name of **the Lord** Jesus Christ. Then they besought him to remain with them certain days.

CHAPTER XI

Now it was heard by the apostles and the brethren that were in Judaea that the Gentiles also had received the word of God. Peter **therefore for a considerable time wished to journey to Jerusalem; and he called to him the brethren, and stablished them; making a long speech, and teaching them throughout the villages: he also went to meet them, and he reported to them the grace of** God. But **the brethren** that were of the circumcision contended with him, saying, Thou wentest in to men uncircumcised, and didst eat with them. But Peter began, and expounded the matter unto them in order, saying, I was in the city of Joppa praying; and in a trance I saw a vision, a certain vessel descending, as it were a great sheet let down from heaven by four corners, and it came even unto me. Upon the which when I had fastened mine eyes, I considered, and saw [the] fourfooted beasts of the earth, and the wild beasts, and creeping things, and fowls of the heaven. And I heard [also] a voice saying unto me, Rise, Peter, kill and eat. But I said, Not so, Lord; for nothing common or unclean hath ever entered into my mouth. But **there was** a voice to **me** [the second time] out of heaven, What God hath cleansed, make not thou common. And this was done thrice; and all were drawn up again into heaven. And behold, forthwith three men stood before the house in which we were, having been sent from Caesarea unto me. And the Spirit bade me go with them [making no distinction]. And these six brethren also accompanied me; and we entered into the man's house; and he told us how he had seen an angel standing in his house, and saying **to him,** Send to Joppa and fetch Simon, whose surname is Peter, who shall speak unto thee words whereby thou shalt be saved, thou and all thy house. And as I began to speak **to them,** the Holy Spirit fell on them, even as on us at the beginning. And I remembered the word of the Lord, how that he said, John indeed baptized with water; but ye shall be baptized with the Holy Spirit. If then [God] gave unto them the like gift as he did also unto us, when we believed on the Lord Jesus Christ, who was I that I could withstand God? **that I should not give them the Holy Spirit when they believed on him.** And when they heard these things, they held their peace; and glorified God, saying, Then to the Gentiles also hath God given repentance unto life.

They therefore that were scattered abroad upon the tribulation that arose from Stephen travelled as far as Phoenicia and Cyprus and Antioch, speaking the word to none save only to Jews. But there were some of them, men of Cyprus and Cyrene, who, when they were come to Antioch spake unto the Greeks [also], preaching the Lord Jesus **Christ**. And the hand of the Lord was with them: and a great number that believed turned unto the Lord. And the report concerning them came to the ears of the Church which was in Jerusalem: and they sent forth Barnabas **that he should go** as far as Antioch; who **also,** when he had come, and had seen the grace of God, was glad; and exhorted them all, that with purpose of heart they would cleave unto the Lord; for he was a good man, and full of the Holy Spirit and of faith: and much people was added unto the Lord.

And **having heard that Saul was at Tarsus,** he went out to seek him; and when he met him he **exhorted him** to come to Antioch.

And they, **when they had** come, for a whole year were gathered together (in the church, and taught) much people, and the disciples were called Christians **then** first in Antioch.

Now in these days there came down prophets from Jerusalem unto Antioch. **And there was much rejoicing; and when we were gathered together** one of them named Agabus stood up and spake, signifying by the Spirit that there should be a great famine over all the world; which came to pass in the days of Claudius. And the disciples, every man according to his ability, determined to send for ministry unto the brethren who dwelt in Judaea; which also they did, sending it to the elders by the hand of Barnabas and Saul.

CHAPTER XII

Now about that time Herod the king put forth his hands to afflict certain of the Church **in Judaea.** And he killed James the brother of John with the sword. And when he saw that **his laying hands upon the faithful** pleased the Jews, he proceeded to seize Peter also. And those were the days of unleavened bread. And when he had taken him, he put him in prison, and delivered him to four quaternions of soldiers to guard him; intending after the Passover to bring him forth to the people. Peter therefore was kept in the prison: but **much** prayer in earnestness **about him** was made by the church to God about him. And when Herod was about to bring him forth, the same night Peter was sleeping between two soldiers, bound with two chains, and guards before the door were keeping the prison. And behold an angel of the Lord stood by **Peter,** and a light shined in the cell; and he **nudged** Peter on the side, and awoke him, saying, Rise up quickly. And his chains fell off from his hands. And the angel said unto him, Gird thyself, and bind on thy sandals. And he did so. And he saith unto him, Cast thy garment about thee and follow me. And he went out and followed; and he wist not that it was true which was done by the angel; **for** he thought he saw a vision. And when they were past the first and the second ward, they came unto the iron gate that leadeth into the city, which opened to them of its own accord, and they went out, **and went down the seven steps,** and passed on through one street; and straightway the angel departed from him. And when Peter was come to himself, he said, Now I know of a truth, that the Lord hath sent forth his angel and delivered me out of the hand of Herod, and from all the expectation of the people of the Jews. And when he had considered the thing, he came to the house of Mary the mother of John, whose surname was Mark: where many were gathered together and were praying. And when he knocked at the door of the gate, a maid came to answer, named Rhoda. And when she knew Peter's voice, she opened not the gate for joy, **and** ran in and told that Peter stood before the gate. And they said unto her, Thou art mad. But she confidently affirmed that it was even so. And they said **Perchance** it is his angel. But Peter continued knocking. And when they had opened and saw him, they were astonished. But he, beckoning unto them with the hand to hold their peace, **came in** and declared unto them how that the Lord had brought him forth out of the prison. And he said, Tell these things unto James, and to the brethren. And he departed and went to another place. Now as soon as it was day, there was a [no small] stir among the soldiers, what was become of Peter. And when Herod had sought for him, and found him not, he examined the guards, and commanded that they should be put to death. And he went down from Judaea to Caesarea, and tarried there.

For he was highly displeased with them of Tyre and Sidon: **but** they with one accord **from both the cities** came **to the king,** and having persuaded Blastus the king's chamberlain, they asked for peace, because their country was fed from the king's country. And upon a set day Herod arrayed himself in royal apparel, and sat on the throne, and made an oration unto them, **after being reconciled with the Tyrians.** And the people shouted, saying, The voice of a god, and not of a man. And immediately an angel of the Lord smote him, because he gave not God the glory. **And he came down from the throne, and while he was still living** he was eaten of worms, and **thus** gave up the ghost.

But the word of God grew and multiplied. And Barnabas and Saul returned from Jerusalem when they had fulfilled their ministration, taking with them John, whose surname was Mark.

CHAPTER XIII

Now there were at Antioch, in the church that was there, prophets and teachers, **among whom were** Barnabas, and Symeon that was called Niger, and Lucius of Cyrene, and Manaen, the foster-brother of Herod the tetrarch, and Saul. And as they ministered to the Lord, and fasted, the Holy Spirit said, Separate me Barnabas and Saul for the work whereunto I have called them. Then when they had **all** fasted and prayed, and had laid their hands on them, [they sent them away.]

So they, being sent forth by the Holy Spirit, went down to Seleucia; and from thence they sailed to Cyprus. And when they were at Salamis, they proclaimed the word **of** the Lord in the Synagogues of the Jews; and they had also John as their attendant. And when they had gone through the whole island unto Paphos, they found a certain sorcerer, a false prophet, a Jew, whose name was Barjesus, which was with the proconsul, Sergius Paulus, a man of understanding. The same called unto him Barnabas and Saul, and sought to hear the word of God. But **Etimas** the sorcerer (for so is his name by interpretation) withstood them, seeking to turn aside the proconsul from the faith, **since he was hearing them with the greatest pleasure.** But Saul who is also called Paul, filled with the Holy Spirit, fastened his eyes on him, and said, O full of all guile and all villany, thou son of the devil, thou enemy of all righteousness, wilt thou not cease to pervert the ways of the Lord **which are** right. And now, behold, the hand of the Lord is upon thee, and thou shalt be blind, not seeing the sun for a season. And immediately there fell on him a mist and a darkness: and he went about seeking some to lead him by the hand. And [then] the proconsul, when he saw what was done **marvelled**, and believed **in God,** being astonished at the teaching of the Lord.

Now Paul and his company set sail from Paphos, and came to Perga of Pamphylia; but John departed from them and returned to Jerusalem. But they, passing through from Perga, came to Antioch of Pisidia; and they went into the synagogue on the Sabbath day, and sat down. And after the reading of the law and the prophets the rulers of the synagogue sent unto them, saying, **Men and** brethren, if ye have any word **of wisdom** of exhortation for the people, say on. And Paul stood up and beckoning with the hand said, Men of Israel, and ye that fear God, hearken. The God of this people Israel chose our fathers and exalted the people when they sojourned in the land of Egypt, and with a high arm led he them forth out of it, and for [about] forty years suffered he their manners in the wilderness. And when he had destroyed seven nations in the land of Canaan, he gave them the land **of the Philistines** for an inheritance; and for about four hundred and fifty years he gave them judges until Samuel the prophet. And afterwards they asked for a king: and God gave unto them Saul, the son of Kish, a man of the tribe of Benjamin, for the space of forty years. And when he had removed him, he raised up David to be their king: to whom also he bare witness, and said, I have found David the son of Jesse, a man after my heart, who shall do all my will. Of this man's seed **therefore** hath God according to promise **raised up** unto Israel a Saviour, Jesus; when John had first preached before his coming the baptism of repentance to all the people of Israel. And as John was fulfilling his course, he said, **Whom** suppose ye that I am? I am not he. But, behold, there cometh one after me, the shoes of whose feet I am not worthy to unloose. **Men and** brethren, children of the stock of Abraham, and those among **us** who fear God, to us is the word of this salvation sent forth. For they that dwell at Jerusalem, and their rulers, [because they knew him not,] nor understanding the **writings** of the prophets which are read every Sabbath, fulfilled them by condemning him. And though they found no cause of death in him, **after judging him they delivered him** to Pilate that he should be slain. And when they had fulfilled all things that were written of him **they asked Pilate to crucify him.** And **when they had obtained this also,** they took him down from the tree, and laid him in a tomb; **whom** God raised from the dead. He was seen for many days of them that came up with him from Galilee to Jerusalem, who **till now** are his witnesses unto the people. And we bring you good tidings of the promise made unto the fathers, that God hath fulfilled the same unto our children, in that he raised up the **Lord** Jesus **Christ. For thus** it is written in the **first** Psalm,

> *Thou art my Son;*
> *this day have I begotten thee*
> **Ask of me and I will give thee the heathen**
> **for thine inheritance,**
> **and the ends of the earth**
> **for thy possession.**

And when he raised him up from the dead, now no more to return to corruption, he hath spoken on this wise, I will give you the holy and sure blessings of David. And elsewhere he saith, Thou wilt not give thy Holy One to see corruption. For David, after he had in his own generation served the counsel of God, fell on sleep, and was laid unto his fathers, and saw corruption; but he whom God raised up saw no corruption. Be it known unto you therefore, **men and** brethren, that through this man is proclaimed unto you remission of sins; and **repentance** from all things from which ye could not be justified by the law of Moses. In him **therefore** every one that believeth is justified **before God.** Beware therefore lest that come upon you which is spoken in the prophets; Behold ye despisers and wonder and vanish away; for I work a work in your days. [a work] which ye shall in no wise believe if a man declare it unto you. **And they kept silence.**

And as they went out, they besought that these words might be spoken to them the next Sabbath. Now when the synagogue broke up, many of the Jews and of the devout proselytes followed Paul and Barnabas; who speaking to them urged them to continue in the grace of God. **And it came to pass that the word of God went throughout the whole city.**

And the next Sabbath almost the whole city was gathered together to hear **Paul telling about the Lord in many words.** And when the Jews saw the multitudes, they were filled with jealousy, and contradicted the words which were spoken by Paul, **contradicting and railing.** And Paul and Barnabas spake out boldly **unto them,** and said, It was **right** that the word of God should first be spoken to you: but seeing ye thrust it from you, and judge yourselves unworthy of eternal life, lo, we turn to the Gentiles. For so hath the Lord commanded [us] saying, I have set thee for a light of the Gentiles, that thou shouldest be for salvation unto the uttermost part of the earth.

And as the Gentiles heard this, they were glad, and they **received** the word of God: and as many as were ordained to eternal life believed. And the word of the Lord was spread abroad throughout all the region. But the Jews urged on the devout women of honourable estate, and the chief men of the city, and stirred up a **great affliction and** persecution against Paul and Barnabas, and cast them out of their borders. But they shook off the dust of their feet against them, and went down to Iconium. And the disciples were filled with joy and with the Holy Spirit.

CHAPTER XIV

And it came to pass in Iconium that **in the same way** he entered into the synagogue of the Jews, and so spake **to them** that a great multitude both of Jews and of Greeks believed. But the rulers of the synagogue of the Jews [that were disobedient] **and the chief men of the synagogue raised up among them** a persecution against the just, and made the souls of the Gentiles evil affected against the brethren. **But the Lord speedily gave them peace.**

Long time therefore they tarried there, speaking boldly in the Lord, which bare witness unto the word of his grace, granting signs and wonders to be done by their hands. But the multitude of the city was divided, and part held with the Jews, and part with the apostles, **cleaving to them on account of the word of God.** And when there was made an onset both of the Gentiles and of the Jews with their rulers to entreat them shamefully and to stone them, they became aware of it, and fled into the cities of Lycaonia, **to** Lystra and Derbe, and **the whole** region round about. And there they preached the gospel. **And the whole multitude was moved at the teaching.**

Now Paul and Barnabas spent some **time at Lystra.** And there sat a certain man impotent in his feet, [a cripple] from his mother's womb, who never had walked. The same heard Paul speaking, **being in fear. And Paul,** fastening his eyes upon him, and seeing that he had faith to be saved, said with a loud voice, **I say to thee in the name of the Lord Jesus Christ,** Stand upright on thy feet, **and walk.** And **straightway suddenly** he leaped up and walked. And when the multitudes saw what Paul had done, they lifted up their voice, saying in the speech of Lycaonia, The gods are come down to us in the likeness of men. And they called Barnabas, Zeus: and Paul, Hermes, because he was the chief speaker. And the **priests** of Zeus, whose temple was before the city, brought **for them** oxen and garlands unto the gates, and would have done sacrifice with the multitudes. But when [the apostles], Barnabas and Paul, heard of it, they rent their garments, and sprang forth among the multitude, crying out and **exclaiming,** Sirs, why do ye these things? We also are men of like passions with you, and bring you good tidings of **God,** that ye should turn from these vain things unto the living God, who made the heaven and the earth and the sea, and all that in them is; who in the generations gone by suffered [all] the nations to walk in their own ways. And yet he left not himself without witness, in that he did good, and gave you from heaven rains and fruitful seasons, filling your hearts with food and gladness. And with those sayings scarce restrained they the multitudes from doing sacrifice unto them. [But] **while they were spending some time there and teaching** there came **certain** Jews from Iconium and Antioch: and having persuaded the multitudes, they stoned Paul, and dragged him out of the city, supposing that he was dead. But as the disciples stood round about him, he rose up, and entered into the city **of Lystra,** and on the morrow he went forth with Barnabas to Derbe. And when they had preached the gospel **to those in** the city, and had made many disciples, they returned to Lystra and to Iconium and to Antioch, confirming the souls of the disciples, **and** exhorting them to continue in the faith, and that through many tribulations we must enter into the kingdom of God. And when they had appointed for them elders in every church, and had prayed with fastings, they commended them to the Lord on whom they had believed. And they passed through Pisidia, and came to Pamphylia. And when they had spoken the word in Perga, they went down to Attalia, **preaching to them the good tidings.** And thence they sailed to Antioch, from whence they had been committed to the grace of God for the work which they had fulfilled. And when they were come, and had gathered the church together, they rehearsed all things that God had done for them **with their souls,** and that he had opened a door of faith unto the Gentiles. And they tarried no little time with the disciples.

CHAPTER XV

And certain men came down from Judaea and were teaching the brethren, saying, Except ye be circumcised **and walk** after the custom of Moses, ye cannot be saved. And Paul and Barnabas had no small dissension and questioning with them, **for Paul spake strongly maintaining that they should remain so as when they believed; but those who had come from Jerusalem,** charged them, Paul and Barnabas and certain others [of them], to go up to Jerusalem unto the apostles and elders **that they might be judged before them** about this question. They therefore, being brought on their way by the Church, passed through both Phoenicia and Samaria, declaring the conversion of the Gentiles; and they caused great joy to all the brethren. And when they were come to Jerusalem, they were received **in great fashion** by the Church and the apostles and the elders, and they rehearsed all things that God had done with them. But **those who had charged them to go up to the elders, being** certain of the sect of the Pharisees who believed, rose up saying, It is needful to circumcise them, and to charge them to keep the law of Moses.

And the apostles and elders were gathered together to consider of this matter. And when there had been much questioning, Peter rose up **in the Spirit** and said unto them, **Men and** brethren, ye know how that a good while ago God made choice among **us** that by my mouth the Gentiles should hear the word of the Gospel and believe. And God, which knoweth the heart, bare them witness, giving **upon** them the Holy Spirit, even as he did unto us; and he made no distinction between us and them, cleansing their hearts by faith. Now therefore why tempt ye God, that ye shall put a yoke upon the neck of the disciples, which neither our fathers nor we were able to bear? But we believe that we shall be saved through the grace of the Lord Jesus **Christ,** in like manner as they.

And the elders agreed to what had been spoken by Peter: and all the multitude kept silence; and they hearkened unto Barnabas and Paul rehearsing what signs and wonders God had wrought among the Gentiles by them. And after they had held their peace, James **rose up and** said, **Men and** brethren, hearken unto me: Symeon hath rehearsed how first God did visit the Gentiles, to take out of them a people for his name. And to this agree the words of the prophets, as it is written,

> *After these things I will return,*
> *And I will build again the tabernacle of David which is fallen;*
> *And I will build again the ruins thereof,*
> *And I will set it up;*
> *That the residue of men may seek after the Lord,*
> *And all the Gentiles upon whom my name is called*
> *Saith the Lord who doeth these things.*
> *Known* **unto the Lord** *from the beginning is his work.*

Wherefore my judgment is that we trouble not them which from among the Gentiles turn to God: but that we enjoin on them to abstain from the pollutions of idols, and from fornication, [and from what is strangled] and from blood: **and that whatsoever they would not should be done to them ye do not to others.** For Moses from generations of old hath in every city them that preach him, being read in the synagogues every Sabbath.

Then it seemed good to the apostles and elders, with the whole church, to choose men out of their company and send them to Antioch with Paul and Barnabas, Judas called **Barabbas,** and Silas, chief men among the brethren. And they wrote **a letter by their hands containing as follows.** The apostles and the elder brethren unto the brethren which are of the Gentiles in Antioch and

Syria and Cilicia, greeting: Forasmuch as we have heard that certain which went out from us have troubled you with words, subverting your souls; to whom we gave no commandment; it seemed good unto us, having come to one accord, to choose out men, and send them to you with **your** beloved Barnabas and Paul, men that have hazarded their lives for the name of our Lord Jesus Christ **in every trial.** We have sent therefore Judas and Silas, who themselves also shall tell you the same things by word of mouth. For it seemed good to the Holy Spirit and to us, to lay upon you no greater burden than these necessary things; that ye abstain from idol sacrifices, and from blood, [and from things strangled], and from fornication **and whatsoever ye would not should be done to yourselves, ye do not to another.** From which if ye keep yourselves ye do well, **being sustained by the Holy Spirit.** Fare ye well.

So they, when they were dismissed, **in a few days** came down to Antioch; and having gathered the multitude together, they delivered the epistle. And when they had read it they rejoiced for the consolation. And Judas and Silas, being themselves also prophets, **full of the Holy Spirit** exhorted the brethren by [much] speech, and confirmed them. And after they had spent some time there, they were dismissed in peace from the brethren unto those that had sent them forth. **But it seemed good to Silas to abide there, and Judas journeyed alone.** But Paul and Barnabas tarried in Antioch, teaching and preaching the word of the Lord, with many others also.

And after some days Paul said to Barnabas, Let us return now and visit the brethren in every city wherein we proclaimed the word of the Lord, and see how they fare. And Barnabas was minded to take with them John [also] who was called Mark. But Paul **was not willing: saying that one who withdrew from them from Pamphylia,** and went not with them to the work **for which they**

were sent, should not be with them. And there arose a sharp contention, so that they parted asunder one from the other. **Then** Barnabas took Mark and sailed to Cyprus; but Paul chose Silas, and went forth, being commended by the brethren to the grace of the Lord. And he went through Syria and Cilicia confirming the churches, **giving to them the commands of the elders.**

CHAPTER XVI

And having passed through these nations he came down to Derbe and Lystra, and, behold, a certain disciple was there, named Timothy, the son of a Jewess which believed; but his father was a Greek. The same was well reported of by the brethren that were at Lystra and Iconium. Him would Paul have to go forth with him; and he took and circumcised him because of the Jews that were in those parts: for they all knew that his father was a Greek. And as they went through the cities **they preached and delivered unto them, with all boldness, the Lord Jesus Christ,** and **at the same time also** delivered [them] the decrees [which had been ordained] of the apostles and elders that were at Jerusalem. So the churches were strengthened [in the faith], and increased in number daily.

And they went through the region of Phrygia and Galatia, having been forbidden of the Holy Spirit to speak the word **of God to any one** in Asia. And when they were come over against Mysia, they **wished** to go into Bithynia, and the Spirit **of Jesus** suffered them not. And passing **through** Mysia, they came down to Troas. And **in** a vision by night there appeared to Paul, **as it were** a certain man of Macedonia, standing **before his face,** beseeching him, and saying, Come over into Macedonia, and help us. When **therefore he had risen up, he related to us the vision,** and we perceived that **the Lord** had called us to preach the Gospel to those who were in Macedonia.

And on the morrow [therefore] we set sail from Troas, and came with a straight course to Samothrace, and the day following to Neapolis; and from thence to Philippi, which is **the capital** of Macedonia, a city, a colony. And we were in this city tarrying certain days. And on the Sabbath day we went forth without the gate by **the** riverside, where **it seemed likely** that there would be a place of prayer: and we sat down, and spake unto the women which were come together. And a certain woman named Lydia, a seller of purple of the city of Thyatira, one that worshipped God, heard us; whose heart the Lord opened to give heed unto the things which were spoken by Paul. And when she was baptized, and **all** her household, she besought us, saying, If ye have judged me to be faithful to **God,** come into my house, and abide there. And she constrained us.

And it came to pass, as we were going to the place of prayer, that a certain maid, having a spirit of divination, met us, which brought her masters much gain **through this,** by soothsaying. The same following after Paul and us cried out saying, These men are servants of the Most High God, who proclaim unto you **the good news of** the way of salvation. And this she did for many days. But Paul, **in the Spirit,** turned, and being sore troubled he said, I charge thee in the name of Jesus Christ, that thou come out of her. And **straightway** it came out.

But when the masters **of the maiden** saw that they **were deprived of the gain which they had through her,** they laid hold on Paul and Silas, and dragged them into the market place before the rulers; and when they had brought them unto the magistrates, they said, These men, being Jews, do exceedingly trouble our city, and set forth customs which it is not lawful for us to receive or to observe, being Romans. And a **great** multitude rose up together against them, **crying out.** Then the magistrates rent their garments off them, and commanded to beat them with rods. And when they had laid many stripes upon them, they cast them into prison, charging the jailer to keep them safely. And he, having received such a charge, cast them into the inner prison, and made their feet fast in the stocks. But about midnight Paul and Silas were praying and singing hymns unto God, and the prisoners were listening to them;

and suddenly there was a great earthquake, so that the foundations of the prison house were shaken; and immediately all the doors were opened, and every one's bands were loosed. And the jailer being roused out of sleep, and seeing the prison doors open, drew his sword, and was about to kill himself, supposing that the prisoners had escaped. But Paul cried with a loud voice, saying, Do thyself no harm; for we are all here. And he called for lights, and sprang in, and trembling for fear, fell down before **the feet of** Paul and Silas, and led them out **after securing the rest,** and said, Sirs, what must I do to be saved? And they said, Believe on the Lord Jesus **Christ,** and thou shalt be saved, thou and thy house. And they spake to him the word of the Lord, with all that were in his house. And he took them the same hour of the night, and washed their stripes, and was baptized, he and all his, immediately. And he brought them into his house, and set meat before them, and rejoiced [greatly] with [all] his house, having believed in God.

But when it was day the magistrates **assembled together into the market place, and recollecting the earthquake that had happened they were afraid; and they** sent the Serjeants, saying, Let those men go **whom yesterday thou didst receive.** And the jailer **came** in, and reported the words to Paul, that, The magistrates have sent to let you go: now therefore come forth, and go on your journey [in peace.] But Paul said unto them, **Without fault alleged** they have beaten us publicly, uncondemned, men that are Romans, and have cast us into prison: and do they now cast us out privily? Nay, verily; but let them come themselves and bring us out. And the Serjeants reported to the magistrates **themselves** these words **which were spoken for the magistrates;** and when they heard that they were Romans they feared; and they came **with many friends into the prison,** and besought them to go forth, **saying, We did not know about you that ye are just men.** And when they had brought them forth, they besought them, saying, Go forth out of this city, **lest they again assemble against us, crying against you.** And they went out of the prison, and went to Lydia; and when they had seen the brethren, they **reported all the things which the Lord had done for them, and** comforted them and departed.

CHAPTER XVII

Now when they had passed through Amphipolis they **went down** to **Apollonis, and thence** to Thessalonica, where was a synagogue of the Jews: and Paul, as his custom was, went in unto them, [and] for three sabbath days discoursed with them from the Scriptures, opening and alleging that it behoved [the] Christ to suffer, and to rise again from the dead, and that this is Christ, Jesus whom, said he, I proclaim unto you. And some of them were persuaded, and consorted with Paul and Silas, **in the teaching:** and **many** of the devout, **and** of Greeks a great multitude, and women, of the first rank, not a few. But the Jews **who disbelieved assembled** certain vile men of the rabble, [gathering a crowd], and set the city on an uproar, and assaulting the house of Jason, they sought to bring them forth to the people. And when they found them not, they dragged Jason and certain brethren before the rulers of the city, crying out **and saying,** These are they that have turned the world upside down, and have come hither [also]; whom Jason hath received; and these all act contrary to the decrees of Caesar, saying that there is another king, Jesus. And they troubled the rulers of the city and the multitude. **When they had heard** these things, and when they had taken security from Jason and the rest, they let them go. And the brethren immediately sent away Paul and Silas by night unto Beroea, who when they were come thither went into the synagogue of the Jews. Now these were more noble than those in Thessalonica, in that they received the word with all readiness of mind, examining the Scriptures daily, whether these things were so. **Some** therefore of them believed, **but some did not believe;** and **of the Greeks and of those of honourable estate, both men and women, many** believed. But when the Jews from Thessalonica had knowledge that the word of God was proclaimed [of Paul] at Beroea [also], **and that they believed,** they came also thither, and **there did not cease to** stir up and trouble the multitudes. Therefore [immediately] the brethren sent forth Paul to go [as far as] to the sea: but Silas and Timothy abode there still. But they that conducted Paul brought him as far as Athens. **But he passed by Thessaly for he was forbidden to proclaim the word to them,** and receiving a commandment **from Paul** to Silas and Timothy that they should come to him with all speed, they departed.

Now while Paul waited for them at Athens, his spirit was provoked within him, as he beheld the city full of idols. So he discoursed in the synagogue with the Jews and the devout persons, and **with those** in the market place every day with them that met with him. And certain also of the Epicurean and Stoic philosophers encountered him. And some said, What would this babbler say? other some, He seemeth to be a setter forth of strange gods, [because he preached Jesus and the Resurrection]. And **after some days** they took hold of him, and brought him unto the Areopagus, **inquiring and** saying May we know what this new teaching is which is spoken by thee? For thou bringest certain strange things to our ears. We would know therefore what these things mean. Now all the Athenians and the strangers sojourning among them, spent their time in nothing else, but either to tell or to hear some new thing. And Paul stood in the midst of the Areopagus, and said,

Ye men of Athens, in all things I perceive that ye are more than others god-fearing. For as I passed along, and observed the objects of your worship, I found also an altar with the inscription, To an unknown god. What therefore ye worship in ignorance, this set I forth unto you. The God that made the world and all things therein, he, being Lord of heaven and earth, dwelleth not in temples made with hands, neither is he served by men's hands, as though he needed [anything], seeing he himself **gave** to all life and breath and all things. He made of one **blood** every nation of man for to dwell on all the face of the earth; having determined their appointed seasons, **according** to the bound of their habitation; that they should seek **most of all that which is divine,** if haply they might feel after **it, or** find it; though it is not far from each one of us; for in him we live and move, and have our being **day by day.** As certain even of your own [poets] have said, For we are also his offspring. Being then the offspring of God, we ought not to think that the Divine is like unto gold or silver or stone, graven by art and device of man. The times of **this** ignorance therefore God overlooked; but now he declareth to men that they should all everywhere repent, inasmuch as he hath appointed a day to judge the world in righteousness by the man **Jesus** whom he hath ordained; giving assurance unto all men, in that he hath raised him from the dead.

Now when they heard of the resurrection of the dead, some mocked; and others said, We will hear thee concerning this yet again. Thus Paul went out from among them. But certain men clave unto him and believed; among whom also was a **certain** Dionysius **an** Areopagite, [and a woman named Damaris] of honourable estate, and others with them.

CHAPTER XVIII

And [after these things] he departed from Athens and came to Corinth. And having found a certain Jew named Aquila, a man of Pontus by race, lately come from Italy, and his wife Priscilla, because Claudius had commanded all Jews to depart from Rome: **these had come to dwell in Greece; Paul** came unto him, and, because he was of the same trade, abode with them and wrought; [for by their trade they were tentmakers]. And **entering into** the synagogue he discoursed every sabbath, and **introduced the name of the Lord Jesus,** and persuaded not only Jews but also Greeks.

But **then** Silas and Timothy came from Macedonia, Paul was constrained by the word, testifying to the Jews that the **Lord** Jesus was the Christ. **And after there had been much discourse, and the scriptures had been interpreted,** when they opposed themselves and blasphemed, Paul shook out his raiment, and said unto them, Your blood be upon your own head; I am clean **from you,** [from henceforth] now I go to the Gentiles. And he left **Aquila,** and entered into the house of a certain man named [Titus] Justus, one that worshipped God, whose house joined hard to the synagogue. And Crispus, the ruler of the synagogue, believed on the Lord with all his house; and many of the Corinthians hearing believed, and were baptized **believing in God through the name of our Lord Jesus Christ.** And the Lord said unto Paul by night in a vision, Be not afraid, but speak, and hold not thy peace: for I am with thee, and no man shall set on thee to harm thee, for I have much people in this city. And he dwelt **in Corinth** a year and six months, teaching them the word of God.

And when Gallio was proconsul of Achaia. the Jews with one accord rose up, **having talked together amongst themselves** against Paul; **and they laid their hands upon** him,** and brought him before the judgment seat, **crying out, and** saying, This man persuadeth men to worship God contrary to the law. But when Paul was about to open his mouth, Gallio said to the Jews, If it were a matter of wrong or of wicked villany, O ye Jews, reason would that I should bear with you: but if ye are **having an** enquiry about words and names and your own law, look to it yourselves. I am not minded to be a judge of these matters. And he drove them from the judgment seat. And **all the Greeks** took hold of Sosthenes, the ruler of the synagogue, and beat him before the judgment seat. **Then Gallio pretended not to see him**. [And Gallio cared for none of these things.]

And Paul, having tarried after this yet many days took his leave of the brethren, and sailed for Syria, and with him Priscilla and Aquila, having shorn his head in Cenchreae: for he had a vow. And **he** came to Ephesus, and **on the next sabbath** he left them there: but he himself entered into the synagogue, and discoursed with the Jews. And when they asked him to abide a longer time, he consented not; but taking his leave of them, and saying, **I must by all means keep the coming feast day at Jerusalem,** and return unto you if God will, he set sail from Ephesus. And when he had landed at Caesarea, he went up and saluted the Church, and went down to Antioch. And having spent some time there he departed, and went through the region of Galatia and Phrygia in order, stablishing all the disciples. Now a certain Jew named **Apollonius,** an Alexandrian by race, a learned man, came to Ephesus; and he was mighty in the scriptures. He had been instructed **in his own country** in the **word** of the Lord; and being fervent in spirit, he spake and taught carefully the things concerning Jesus, knowing only the baptism of John. He began to speak boldly in the synagogue. But when Aquila and Priscilla heard him, they took him unto them, and expounded the Way [of God] unto him more carefully.

Now certain Corinthians were sojourning in Ephesus, and having heard him, they exhorted him to cross with them into their own country; and when he consented the Ephesians wrote to the disciples in Corinth that they should receive the man. And **when he sojourned in Achaia** he helped them much in **the churches,** for he powerfully confuted the Jews, **reasoning** publicly, and shewing by the scriptures that Jesus was Christ.

CHAPTER XIX

And **when Paul, according to his private wish, desired to go to Jerusalem, the Spirit told him to return into Asia.** And [while Apollos was at Corinth] he passed through the upper districts and **comes** to Ephesus, and found certain disciples; and he said unto them, Did ye receive the Holy Spirit when ye believed? And they said unto him, Nay, we have not even heard (that) **any receive the** Holy Spirit. And he said, Into what then were ye baptized? And they said, Into John's baptism. And Paul said, John baptized with the baptism of repentance, saying unto the people that they should believe on him which should come after him, that is, on **Christ.** And when they heard this they were baptized into the name of the Lord Jesus **Christ, unto the remission of sins.** And when Paul had laid his hand on them **straightway** the Holy Spirit **fell** upon them: and they spake with tongues, and prophesied. And they were in all about twelve men.

And **Paul** entered into the synagogue, and **with great power** spake boldly for the space of three months, discoursing and persuading [as to the things] concerning the kingdom of God. Some **therefore** of them were hardened and unbelieving, and spake evil of the Way before the multitude **of the Gentiles. Then** Paul departed from them, and separated the disciples, discoursing daily in the school of **one** Tyrannus **from the fifth till the tenth hour.** And this continued for [the space of] two years; so that all they that dwelt in Asia heard the words of the Lord, [both] Jews and Greeks. And God wrought special miracles by the hands of Paul; insomuch **even** that unto the sick were carried away from his body handkerchiefs or aprons, and the diseases departed from them, and the evil spirits went out. But certain [also] of the strolling Jews, exorcists, took upon them to name over them which had the evil spirits the name of the Lord Jesus, saying, I adjure you by Jesus whom Paul preacheth. **Among whom also** [were]the [seven] sons of one Sceva, [a Jew] a [chief] priest, [who] **wished to do the same thing, being accustomed to exorcise such people. And they came in unto one who was possessed with a devil, and began to call upon the Name saying, We command you, in Jesus whom Paul preacheth, to come out. Then the evil spirit** answered and said unto them, Jesus I recognise, and Paul I know: but who are ye? And the man in whom the evil spirit was leaped on them, and mastered both of them, and prevailed against them, so that they fled out of that house naked and wounded. And this became known to all, [both] Jews and Greeks, that dwelt at Ephesus; and fear fell upon them all, and the name of the Lord Jesus was magnified. Many also of them that **were believing,** came confessing and declaring their deeds. And not a few of them that practised curious arts brought also their books together, and burned them in the sight of all: and they counted the prices of them, and found it fifty thousand pieces of silver. So mightily did it prevail; and the **faith of God** increased and **multiplied.**

[Now after these things were ended] then Paul purposed in the Spirit to pass through Macedonia and Achaia, and go to Jerusalem, saying, After I have been there I must also see Rome. And having sent into Macedonia two of them that ministered unto him, Timothy and Erastus, he himself stayed for a **little** while in Asia.

And about that time there arose no small stir about the Way. For there was a certain man [named] Demetrius, a silversmith, which made silver shrines of Diana, **who** brought no little business unto the craftsmen. He gathered together the craftsmen of such things, and said unto them, Fellow craftsmen, ye know that out of this business we have our wealth. And ye hear and see that not alone at

Ephesus, but almost throughout all Asia, this Paul, **a somebody,** hath persuaded and turned away much people, saying that they be no gods which are made with hands: and not only is there danger that this our trade come into disrepute; but also that the temple of the great goddess Diana be made of no account, but is about to be deposed [from her magnificence, whom] all Asia and the world worshippeth. And when they heard this, they were filled with wrath, **and they ran into the street,** and cried out saying, Great is Diana of the Ephesians. And the whole city was filled with confusion, and they rushed with one accord into the theatre, having seized Gaius and Aristarchus, men of Macedonia, Paul's companions in travel. And when Paul was minded to enter in unto the people, the disciples suffered him not. And certain also of the chief officers of Asia, being his friends, sent unto him, and besought him not to adventure himself into the theatre. Some therefore cried one thing and some another; for the assembly was in confusion; and the more part knew not wherefore they were come together. And they brought Alexander out of the crowd, the Jews putting him forward. And Alexander beckoned with the hand, and would have made a defence unto the people. But when they perceived that he was a Jew, all with one voice about the space of two hours cried out, Great is Diana of the Ephesians. But the townclerk **beckoned** to the crowd and saith, Ye men of Ephesus, what man is there who knoweth not how that **our** city is temple-keeper of the great Diana, and of the image which fell down from Jupiter? Seeing then that these things cannot be gainsaid, ye ought to be quiet, and to do nothing rash. For ye have brought hither these men, which are neither robbers of temples nor blasphemers of our goddess.

If therefore this Demetrius, and the craftsmen that are with him, have **any** matter against **them,** the courts are open, and there are proconsuls; let them accuse one another.

But if ye seek anything about other matters, it shall be settled **according to the law of** the assembly. For indeed we are in danger this day to be accused of riot, there being no cause for which we shall be able to give an account of this concourse. And when he had thus spoken he dismissed the assembly.

CHAPTER XX

And after the uproar was ceased, Paul having sent for the disciples, and given them **much** exhortation, took leave of them and departed [for to go] into Macedonia. And when he had gone through those parts, and had given them much exhortation, he came into Greece. And when he had spent three months there, and a plot was laid against him by the Jews he **wished** to sail for Syria. **But the Spirit said to him** to return through Macedonia, **therefore when he was about to go out** as far as Asia, Sopater of Beroea, the son of Pyrrhus; and of the Thessalonians Aristarchus and Secundus, and Gaius of Derbe, and Timothy: and **of Ephesians Eutychus** and Trophimus. These had gone before and were waiting for **him** at Troas. But we sailed away from Philippi after the days of unleavened bread, and came unto them to Troas in five days; where we tarried seven days. And upon the first day of the week, when we were gathered together to break bread, Paul discoursed with them intending to depart on the morrow, and prolonged his speech until midnight. And there were many lights in the upper chamber, where we were gathered together. And there sat in the window a certain young man named Eutychus, borne down with deep sleep; and as Paul discoursed yet longer, being borne down by his sleep, he fell down from the third storey and was taken up dead. And Paul went down, and fell on him, and embracing him said, Make ye no ado, for his life is in him. And when he was gone up, and had broken the bread, and had eaten, and had talked with them a long while, even till break of day, so he departed. And **as they were bidding him farewell** they brought the young man alive, and were not a little comforted.

But we went down to the ship, and set sail for Assos, there intending to take in Paul. For so had he appointed, **as** intending himself to go on foot. And, when he met us at Assos, we took him in, and came to Mitylene. And sailing from thence we came the following day over against Chios; and the next day we touched at Samos, **and tarried at Trogyllium:** and the day after we came to Miletus. For Paul had determined to sail past Ephesus: lest some **detention for him might occur** in Asia, for he was hastening [if it were possible for him] to be in Jerusalem on the day of Pentecost.

And from Miletus he sent to Ephesus, and **sent for** the elders of the Church. And when they were come to him, **and were together,** he said unto them, Ye yourselves know, **brethren,** from the first day that I set foot in Asia, **for three years and even more,** after what manner I was with you all the time, serving the Lord, with all lowliness of mind, and with tears, and with trials which befell me by the plots of the Jews: how that I shrank not from declaring unto you all that was profitable, and from teaching from house to house and publicly, testifying both to Jews and to Greeks repentance toward God, and faith **through** our Lord Jesus Christ. And now, behold, I go bound in the spirit unto Jerusalem, not knowing the things which shall befall me there, save that the Holy Spirit testifieth unto me in every city saying that bonds and afflictions abide me in Jerusalem. But I take account of none of these things, nor hold my life as dear unto myself, that I may accomplish my course and the ministry **of the word** which I received from the Lord Jesus to testify **to Jews and Greeks** the gospel of the grace of God. And now, behold, I know, that ye all among whom I went about preaching the kingdom **of Jesus** shall see my face no more. Therefore [I testify unto you that] **until** this day I am pure from the blood of all men. For I shrank not from declaring unto you the whole counsel of God. Take heed unto yourselves and to all the flock, in the which the Holy Spirit hath made you bishops, to feed the Church of **the Lord** which he purchased for himself with his own blood. I know that after my departing grievous wolves shall enter in among you, not sparing the flock; and from among your own selves shall men arise, speaking perverse things, to draw away the disciples after them. Wherefore watch ye, remembering that by the space of three years I ceased not to admonish every one night and day with tears. And now I commend you to God, and to the word of his grace, which is able to build you up, and to give you inheritance among [all] them that are sanctified. I coveted **of you all** no man's silver, or gold, or apparel. Ye yourselves know that my hands ministered unto my necessities, and to [all] them that were with me. In all things I gave you an example, that so labouring ye ought to help the weak, [and] to remember the words of the Lord Jesus how that he himself said, It is more blessed to give than to receive.

And when he had thus spoken, he kneeled down, and prayed with them all. And they all wept sore, and fell on Paul's neck, and kissed him; sorrowing most of all for the word which he spake, Ye shall see my face no more. And they brought him on his way unto the ship.

CHAPTER XXI

And when [it came to pass that] we had set sail and were parted from them, we came with a straight course unto Cos, and the next day unto Rhodes, and from thence unto Patara **and Myra;** and having found a ship crossing unto Phoenice.

One leaf is missing here, containing xx. 31 to xxi. 2 in Latin, and xxi. 2-10 in Greek.

...prophet named Agabus. And coming up to us, and taking Paul's girdle, he bound his own feet and hands, and said, Thus saith the Holy Spirit, so shall the Jews at Jerusalem bind the man that owneth this girdle, and shall deliver him into the hands of the Gentiles. And when we heard these things, both we and they of that place besought **Paul** not **himself** to go up to Jerusalem. But Paul said to us, What do ye, weeping and **disturbing** my heart; for I **desire** not to be bound only but am ready also to die at Jerusalem for the name of the Lord Jesus **Christ.** And when he would not be persuaded, we ceased, saying **to one another,** The will of **God** be done.

And after **certain** days we **bade them farewell,** and we go up to Jerusalem **from Caesarea;** and with us **those who led us to** him with whom we should lodge. And **when they came to a certain village, we stayed with** Nason, a certain Cyprian, an old disciple; and **going forth thence** we came to Jerusalem. And the brethren received us gladly.

And the day following Paul went in with us unto James, and the elders were assembled **with him.** And when he had saluted them he rehearsed one by one the things which God had wrought among the Gentiles by his ministry. And when they heard it they glorified **the Lord,** saying, Thou seest, brother, how many myriads there are **in Judaea** of them which have believed, and they are all zealous for the law; and they have been informed concerning thee, that thou teachest [all] the Jews which are among the Gentiles to forsake Moses, telling them not to circumcise their children, neither to walk after their customs. What is it therefore? **The multitude must needs come together, for** they will hear that thou art come. Do therefore this that we say to thee. We have four men which have a vow on them; these take, and purify thyself with them, and be at charges for them, that they may shave their heads; and all may know that there is no truth in the things whereof they have been informed concerning thee; but that thou thyself also walkest orderly, keeping the law. But as touching the Gentiles which have believed, **they have nothing to say against thee, for** we sent giving judgment, **that they should observe nothing of that sort,** except to guard themselves from idol sacrifices, and from blood, [and from what is strangled], and from fornication. Then Paul took the men, and the next day purifying himself with them he went into the temple, declaring the fulfilment of the days of purification until the offering was made for every one of them.

And when the seven days were [almost] completed, the Jews **who had come** from Asia, when they saw him in the temple, stirred up all the multitudes, and laid hands upon him, crying out, Men of Israel, help: This is the man that teacheth all men everywhere against the people, and the law, and this place; and moreover he brought Greeks into the temple, and hath denied this holy place. For they had before seen with him in the city Trophimus the Ephesian, whom they supposed that Paul had brought into the temple. And all the city was moved, and the people ran together: and they laid hold on Paul, and dragged him out of the temple: and straightway, the doors were shut. And as they were seeking to kill him, tidings came up to the chief captain of the band, that all Jerusalem was in confusion. And forthwith he took soldiers and centurions and ran down upon them: and they, when they saw the chief captain and the soldiers, left beating of Paul. Then the chief captain came near, and laid hold on him, and commanded him to be bound with two chains, and enquired who he was and what he had done. And some shouted one thing, and some another, among the crowd; and when he could not know the certainty for the uproar, he commanded him to be brought into the castle. And when he came upon the stairs, so it was, that he was borne of the soldiers for the violence of the people: for the multitude [of the people] followed after, crying out, Away with him.

And as he was about to be brought into the castle, he **answered and** said to the chief captain, May I speak unto thee? And he said, Dost thou know Greek? Art thou not [then] the Egyptian, which before these days stirred up to sedition, and led out into the wilderness, the four thousand men of the Assassins? But Paul said, I am a Jew, **born in** Tarsus of Cilicia, [a citizen of no mean city], and I beseech thee give me leave to speak unto the people. And when **the chief Captain** had given him leave, Paul, standing on the stairs, beckoned with the hand unto the people: and when there was made a great silence, he spake unto them in the Hebrew language, saying:

CHAPTER XXII

Men, Brethren and fathers, hear ye my defence which I make now unto you. And when they heard that he spake [unto them] in the Hebrew language, they were the more quiet; and he saith, I am a Jew, born in Tarsus of Cilicia, but brought up in this city at the feet of Gamaliel, instructed according to the strict manner of the law of our fathers, zealous for God, even as ye all are this day. And I persecuted this Way unto death, binding and delivering into prison both men and women. As also the high priest **will** bear witness to me, and all the estate of the elders, from whom I received letters from the brethren. I was journeying to Damascus, to bring them also that were there unto Jerusalem in bonds, that they might be punished. And [it came to pass that as I made my journey], as I drew nigh unto Damascus, about noon, suddenly there shone from heaven a great light round about me, and I fell unto the ground, and heard a voice saying unto me, Saul, Saul, why persecutest thou me? And I answered, Who art thou, Lord? And he said unto me, I am Jesus **of Nazareth** whom thou persecutest. And they that were with me saw indeed the light, **and were frightened;** but they heard not the voice of him that spake with me. And I said, What shall I do, Lord. And **he** said unto me, Arise, and go into Damascus, and there it shall be told thee of all things which thou oughtest to do. But **when I rose up** I did not see for the glory of that light, and being led by the hand of them that were with me I came into Damascus. And one Ananias, a devout man according to the law, and by the witness of all the Jews, came unto me and [standing by me] said unto me, **Saul,** Brother Saul, receive thy sight; and in that very hour I received sight. And he said **unto me,** The God of our fathers hath appointed thee to know his will, and to see the Righteous one, and to hear a voice from his mouth; for thou shalt be a witness for him unto all men of what thou hast seen and heard. And now, why tarriest them? Arise, be baptized, and wash away thy sins, calling on his name. And it came to pass that when I had returned to Jerusalem and while I prayed in the temple, I fell into a trance, and saw him saying unto me, Make haste and get thee quickly out of Jerusalem because they will not receive **my** testimony [from thee.] And I said, Lord, they themselves know that I imprisoned and beat in every synagogue them that believed on thee: and when the blood of Stephen the witness was shed, I [also] was standing by, and consenting, and keeping the garments of them that slew him. And he said unto me, Depart, for I send thee forth far hence unto the Gentiles.

And they gave him audience unto this word: and they lifted up their voice and said, Away with such a fellow from the earth, for it is not fit that he should live. And as they cried out, and threw off their garments, and cast dust into the air, the chief captain commanded him to be brought into the castle, bidding that he should be examined by scourging, that he might know for what cause they so shouted against him. And when they had tied him up with the thongs, he said unto the centurion that stood by, Is it lawful for you to scourge a man that is a Roman and uncondemned. And when the centurion heard this, **that he called himself a Roman** he went to the chief captain and told him, **See** what thou art about to do. This man is a Roman. Then the chief captain came **and asked him,** Tell me, art thou a Roman? and he said, I am. And the chief captain answered, **I know** with how great a sum I obtained this citizenship. And Paul said, But I am [a Roman] born. Then they departed from him...

All the rest of the Codex Bezae is wanting.

www.ingramcontent.com/pod-product-compliance
Lightning Source LLC
LaVergne TN
LVHW041458070426
835507LV00009B/662